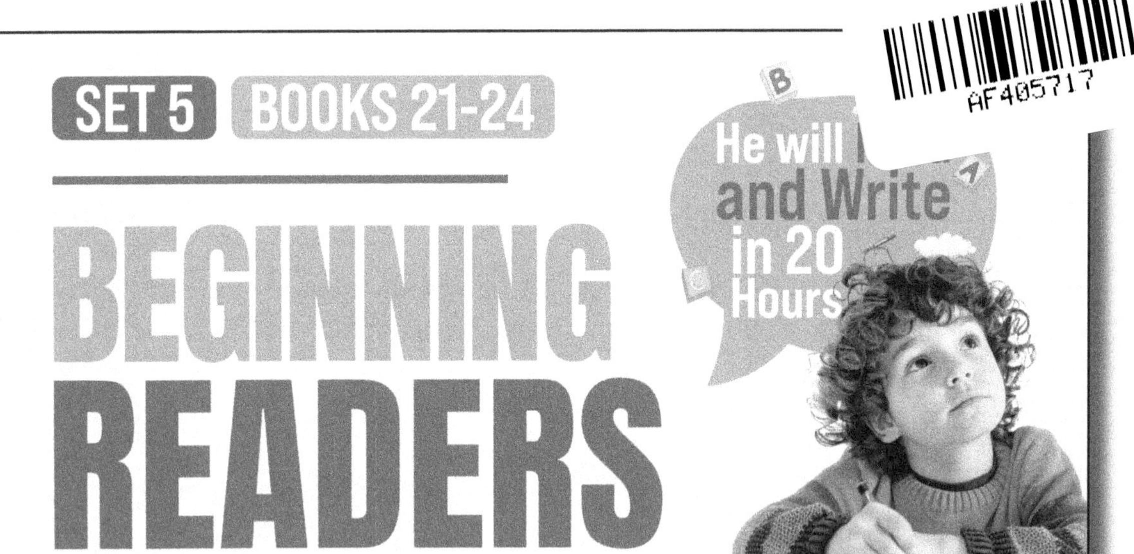

Includes 4 books in 1 set

21. Mitsi's Love
22. Carmela the Camel
23. The Little Witch Who Wasn't Wicked
24. The Sparkly Red Slippers

ANNETTE J. PRIMIANI, B.S., M.S.

Published by Annette J. Primiani. This book contains the exact beginning readers used in The Learning Connection TLC, Inc.'s *He Will Read and Write in 20 Hours* tutoring and home school programs and can be used in conjunction with the main instructional book. For more information visit: **www.LearningConnectionTLCinc.com**

Printed in the United States of America

ISBN: 979-8-9917415-8-3 (softcover)
ISBN: 979-8-9917415-9-0 (ebook)

These books provide a stable foundation for the majority of reading programs in use today. Our reading guarantee is applicable for children who are ready and applying the step-by-step program in our tutoring center. Your results may vary.

Author website: learningconnectiontlcinc.com
Author email: tlcinc@earthlink.net

The manual for teaching your child to read and write

A note from Annette...

"Your child will read and write in 20 hours! We produce results!"

That is the motto of my tutoring center and we have been reaching this goal, using a combination of exact methods, for over 30 years!

This applies to "ready to read" pre-school kids, to kindergarten-aged children and older, and to others who may be functionally illiterate. My tutoring center in Florida, **The Learning Connection TLC, Inc.**, uses this reading program. As of this writing, we have been chosen the Best Tutoring Service in all of Tampa Bay for the last six years!

This book you're holding is Set 5, featuring the fifth group of beginning readers used in the program. Set 1 contains the shortest and easiest stories. It's best to start with Set 1 and continue onwards as your child advances. They allow the student to read words with carefully chosen short vowels and several consonants. There are 5 book sets, each one carrying on with the next gradient step of simple readers for your child. The basic strategy, however, of teaching your child to read remains the same.

These children's books have been reproduced exactly as originally published; that is, one page at a time on a two-page spread. This helps the child to focus on and sound out the words on each single page without distraction.

They are companion books to *He Will Read and Write in 20 Hours*, an easy to understand, step by step book written to teach a child to read if your child is ready. Just with the reading manual and these 5 book sets, you too can achieve results within the 20 hours program of 40 lessons at :30 minutes each.

Why does this program work? I use the "Words in Color" teaching method developed by Dr. Caleb Gattegno as my base and have taken it a step further by writing additional teaching tools such as this book set. Gattegno was a world-renowned educator, known for his methods of teaching reading and math. His programs continue to be used today in select schools seeking literacy excellence for their students.

I am likely one of the few active educators still utilizing Gattegno's system who actually knew, trained and worked with Gattegno. In fact, at one time I lectured and trained other teachers at his New York educational center!

Others in the years since have borrowed from Gattegno's works but I've found from experience that using his system still gets the best results. Additionally, there are many beginning reader books out there, but most with a built-in, inherent problem.

They may be interesting to look at, sometimes with familiar or famous superhero characters, brought vividly to life with color drawings on each page. The action is more exciting to draw the eye than the words! A child also will learn to sight read or memorize a book that has been repeatedly read to him, rather than accurately sounding out the words.

Then there is the matter of the different text fonts used in books; the use of capital letters at the start of sentences; and pronunciation problems such as whether the letter "a", for example, should be a soft vowel pronounced like the "a" in "cat" as opposed to the long vowel pronunciation in the word "hay". Or if the letter looks like this: "**a**" with a curl to it, as opposed to this, a circle and a line: "**ɑ**".

These confusions can easily lead to frustration and failure for a child and put a damper on his enthusiasm for wanting to read at all! This may cause a parent to give up and decide that the child's school can better handle it.

That is why my books have simple, hand-drawn pictures. The beginning stories have all lower case letters in words, and are in black-and-white. The child needs to focus on and read the words to get the full idea of what is happening in the story. You, as the homeschool teacher, can ensure your child is at ease using a step-by-step approach!

Additionally, you want to make certain your child <u>understands</u> the words he or she is reading. In the story "pop's pot" (in Set 1 of the series), the word "pop" means daddy or father. In the story "pop, pop, pop" (in Set 2 of the series), the word "pop" means a soda drink. If your child is unfamiliar with a word or has a wrong definition, be sure to explain the meaning to them as it's used in the story. This ensures your child can fully understand and enjoy what he or she reads.

My goal has always been to help conquer illiteracy. In my early career, I taught in the New York public school system, in the poorest and most crime-ridden areas of the Bronx and Brooklyn. These students generally were not very interested in being educated but they turned around and their test scores improved, to the surprise of the school staff.

Later, I moved to Los Angeles, opened a tutoring center there, and gained a reputation for my success in teaching students from autistic, to gifted pres-schoolers, to adults. During my years as a teacher, the students I tutored ranged from inner city kids who were illiterate or seriously behind grade level, to children of movie stars and celebrities.

For a time, I lived in Mexico City, where I again worked with children and adults, ranging from poorer families to those of the aristocracy, as well as teaching them English as a Second Language. (E.S.L.)

Today, I live in Florida. Our tutoring center additionally offers morning homeschool classes, often to catch students up to grade level or beyond. We have hundreds of success stories from children, parents and students of all ages. You can read some of them on our website: **LearningConnectionTLCInc.com** and also on our Facebook page: **facebook. com/TheLearningConnectionTLC**. You can contact me on the website or Facebook.

By the way, the young boy in the cowboy hat pictured above was one of my tutoring students. He is now a physicist at the NASA Space Center!

One of the joys in life is watching your child learn to read and write their first words. It's such a turning point of growing up and a boost to pride and self-esteem. Enjoy those precious moments and have fun with your child!

Annette

Annette

Vocabulary for Book 21

Best to explain these words:
poodle, noodles, oodles,
stuff herself, master

Mitsi's Love

Mitsi was a poodle.
Mitsi was a funny poodle.

Mitsi loved noodles.
Mitsi loved oodles of
noodles.

Mitsi loved noodle bones, noodle cake, noodle burgers, and noodle buns.

If Mitsi's master gave
Mitsi any other dog food,
Mitsi just stuck up her
nose and turned her head.

4

Mitsi liked to stuff
herself with noodles.
Mitsi ate and ate
and ate and ate.

Mitsi got
bigger
and bigger
and bigger
and bigger.

Soon, Mitsi was not
able to move!

Mitsi was not hungry
for two weeks!

Mitsi still likes noodles, but not as much.
Mitsi likes other food too !

Vocabulary for Book 22

Best to explain these words:

desert, factory, caramel

invented, smooth, bumpy

Carmela the Camel

Most camels have one hump. But _not_ Carmela the camel. Carmela the camel had _two_ humps.

1

The other camels made
fun of Carmela and
her two humps.

Carmela the camel
wished that she was
like the others. She'd
cry and cry and cry !!!

4

One day, King Carmine, the candy king, asked for a smooth riding camel to cross the desert. He had a secret candy that he had just invented. It had to get to his candy factory on the other side of the desert. <u>But</u>, the ride needed to be smooth. A bumpy ride was not very good for the candy.

Carmela had her chance.
She gave the candy a
smooth ride!

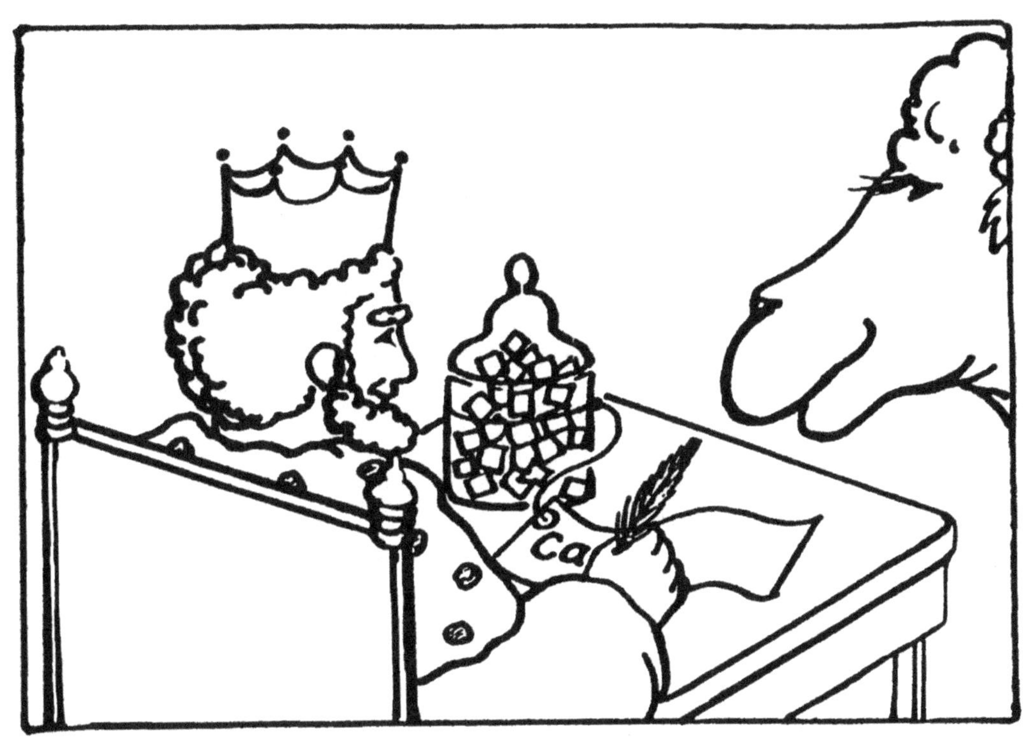

King Carmine was so happy that he named the new candy after Carmela. He named the new candy "caramels."

The other camels cheered for Carmela. The other camels admired her two humps. The others wanted two humps, too!

From then on, Carmela
did not cry and cry and
cry. From then on,
Carmela smiled and
smiled and smiled.

"I like my humps !
I like my humps !
I like my humps !"

Vocabulary for Book 23

Best to explain these words:
wicked, stroller, speeding,
traffic, sudden, rushed

The Little Witch
Who Wasn't Wicked

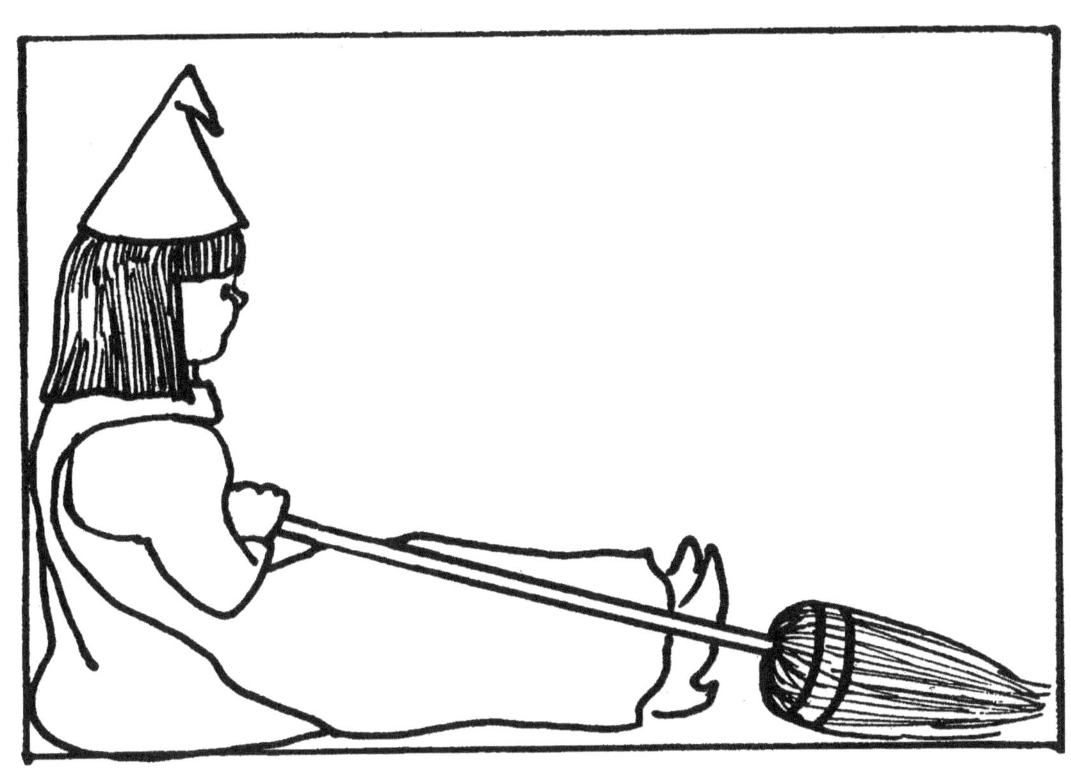

Carlotta was a little witch.

1.

But Carlotta was not like the others. Carlotta was <u>not</u> wicked. Carlotta liked children. Carlotta liked to help. Carlotta liked to fly.

2.

The other witches made fun
of her for being good.
"A good witch?
"There's no such thing!
"You're not even <u>mean</u>!"

3.

Carlotta did not want to stay with the mean witches. Carlotta was <u>not</u> wicked. "I wish the children would play with me. I will ask them."

4.

As soon as she went over to the children, they ran away. They were scared. They didn't know that Carlotta was a good witch. Carlotta felt very unhappy.

5.

All of a sudden Carlotta heard a mother cry for help.

Her child was in a run-away stroller speeding down a big hill. It Kept going faster and faster. It had to be stopped. At the bottom of the hill was traffic!

Carlotta rushed to save her.

Carlotta stopped the stroller just in time. The child was saved !

9.

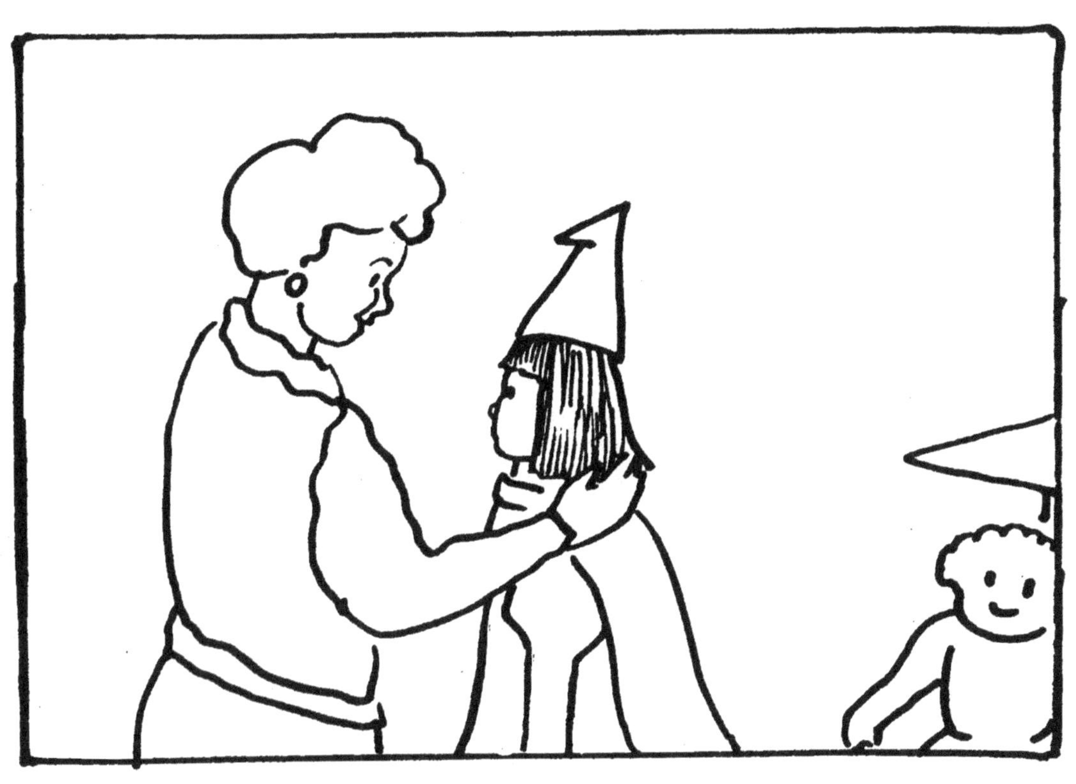

The child's mother was very thankful. She invited Carlotta to her home for dinner.

There was a party for her. There were many children to play with!

11.

This time, the children were not scared. <u>This</u> time, they did not run away! Carlotta was very happy!

12.

Vocabulary for Book 24

Best to explain these words:

sparkly, tantrum, earn, porch, weeds, swept, she'd, wah, $, hollered, tantrum, yippee

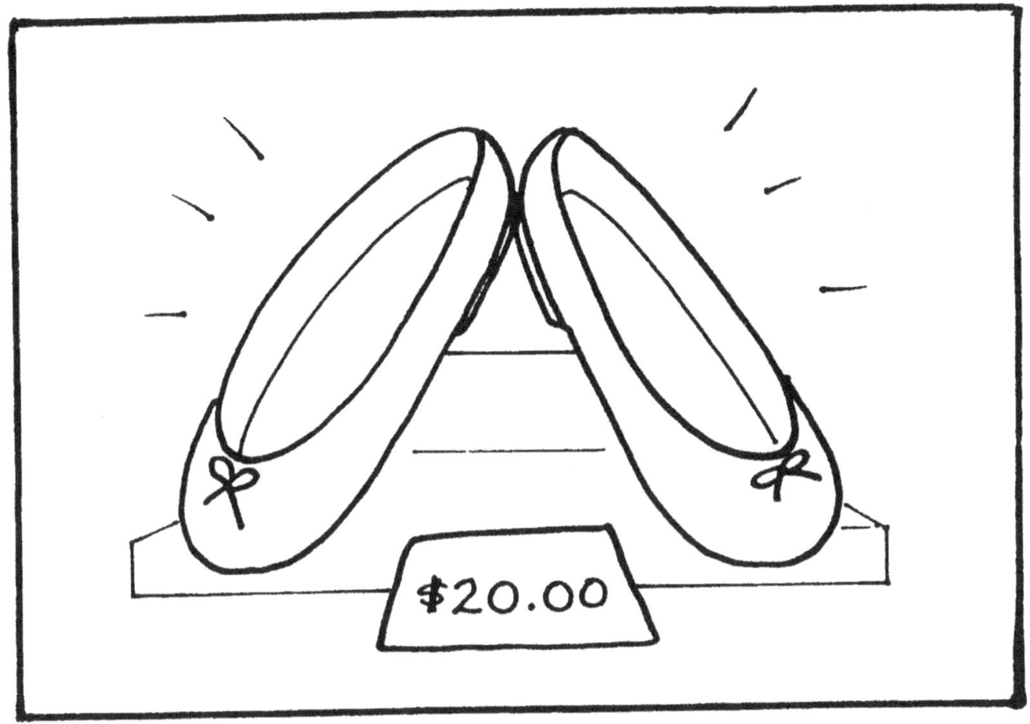

The Sparkly Red Slippers

Suzy looked in the shop window. Her mouth fell open as she saw the beautiful red slippers. The red slippers sparkled.

1.

"Oh! I wish those sparkly
red slippers were mine!
What can I do? I don't
have twenty dollars."

2.

"I will ask my mother."
"Mother, can you get me sparkly, red slippers?"
"No, dear, not today."

3.

"I will ask my father."
"Daddy, can you get me
sparkly, red slippers?"
"No, dear, not today."

4.

"I will ask my grandmother." "Grandma, can you get me sparkly, red slippers?" "No, dear, not today."

5.

Each person Suzy asked said, "No, dear, not today."

Suzy began to cry and cry. Suzy jumped up and down and hollered. Suzy had a tantrum!

Suzy was sent to her room. "Go to your room."

In her room, Suzy had
time to think. She had
an idea. Soon she'd have
those sparkly red slippers.
She'd earn the twenty
dollars herself!   9.

Suzy began to work. She washed the dishes. She took out the garbage. She pulled up the weeds. She washed dad's car. She swept the porch.

10.

Suzy worked and worked and worked. Suzy earned and earned and earned. Suzy smiled and smiled and smiled.

11.

Yippee!
Suzy has her sparkly red
slippers!

12.